Für Familie Lühl
ein lieber Gruß
von Udo Stenck
Mourne Grange
16.2.1998

ONE THOUSAND AND MORE ANIMAL PROVERBS

Udo Steuck

MINERVA PRESS
LONDON
MONTREUX LOS ANGLES SYDNEY

ISBN 1 86106 394 6

First Published 1997 by
MINERVA PRESS
195 Knightsbridge,
London SW7 1RE.

Printed in Great Britain for Minerva Press

ONE THOUSAND AND MORE ANIMAL PROVERBS

About the Author

Udo Steuck was born in a village of a mixed German-Polish population. The place was the German, but now belongs to Poland. His parents and maternal grandparents were always very fond of proverbs and weather lore and applied these extensively to all situations of their lives.

No wonder that Udo Steuck showed a very early interest in proverbs, folklore and languages. As a child, he would try to write down German words in search of their Polish equivalents and also expressions of the West Prussian dialect spoken by his grandparents.

One of his early teachers collected weather lore with the help of his pupils. This educator's dictations were mostly a medley of proverbs.

All this led the author to a lifelong love for the wisdom inherent in various languages. In his studies he found Scottish, English and Irish proverbs especially rewarding.

In September 1951 as a young co-worker, he joined the Camphill Schools near Aberdeen in Scotland. He has been connected with the Camphill Movement ever since, taking up various appointments which led him to make his home in England and Ireland, too.

He was fortunate to undergo in his life a wide range of studies and training. He is a trained teacher, curative teacher (BA, Susan B. Anthony University), farmer with nine years experience (City and Guilds: farm business management) and ordained priest. His hobbies are gardening, beekeeping, piano playing and landscape painting. The silhouettes in this book are contributed by him.

Foreword

Preparing a sequel to One Thousand and More Animal Proverbs, this time concerning plants, I notice how much more difficult it is to find 1000 proverbs of plants.

To see what other languages have to offer I have browsed through these two volumes of German proverbs, each containing more than 15,000 sayings:

Sprichwörter-Lexikon, H. & A. Beyer, Bibliographisches Institut, Leipzig 1985.

Die Deutschen Sprichwörter, collected by Karl Simrock, Philipp Reclam jun., Stuttgart 1995.

I discovered that a large number of German proverbs have their equivalent in English, Scottish and Irish sayings. Further Greek and Latin adages can be found in:

Veni Vidi Vici, chosen and translated by K. Bartels, Deutscher Taschenbuch Verlag, München 1992.

The following Swedish book is to be recommended:

Osed och Ordsed, Per Erik Wahlund, Natur och Kultur, Viborg 1990.

This list ought also to include:

English Proverbs and Proverbial Phrases, G.L. Appersen, J.M. Dent and Sons Ltd, London 1929.

Animal proverbs provide a special attraction. They are like mirrors reflecting our anger and destructiveness, our naivety, pride, lust, but also our love and contentment.

Proverbs played a much greater part in the life of preceding centuries than in the present time. Sure enough, there is more openness and with it tactlessness among us in modern society, and with our frank directness we easily offend.

However, what has to be said can often be conveyed through an objective, fairly inoffensive proverb. This may leave the addressed person pondering about the possible meaning in relation to himself. Most likely it will be easier for him to accept its message thus conveyed.

Proverbs have indeed been invaluable educators of mankind during all those years of their existence. May this book kindle new enthusiasm for the wisdom of past generations expressed in these sayings

I am very grateful for the help I have received in making this edition possible. My thanks go to Fionnuala Williams, author of *The Polbeg Book of Irish Proverbs*, who in a letter, gave me sound advice for a future publication. Many thanks also to both Professors Sèamus Ò. Cathàin and Bo Almquist of University College Dublin (Department of Irish Folklore), who permitted me to include a large number of Irish proverbs in my book.

Obviously I am indebted to all the publishing houses who made this compilation possible, but especially to Minerva Press for this very meticulous and beautiful edition.

Udo Steuck
February 1997

Dedication

I dedicate this book with gratitude to my wife, Lisa,
who always supported me with her infinite patience
during the various stages of my work

Contents

Adder

See also serpent, snake, viper.

If the adder could hear and the blindworm could see neither man nor beast would ever go free.

March comes in with adder heads, and goes out with peacock tails.

March wind wakens the adder and blooms the thorn.

Put your hand in the creel, tak [take] out an adder or an eel.

Ant

An emmet [ant] may work its heart out, but can never make honey.

Even an emmet [ant] may seek revenge. (8)

The ant has wings to her hurt.

The fly has her spleen, and the ant her gall.

Ape

See also monkey.

An ape's an ape, a varlet's a varlet, though they be clad in silk or scarlet. (4)

An old ape has an old eye.

The ape kills her young with kindness. (8)

The higher the ape goes, the more he shows his tail.

You cannot make a horn of an ape's tail.

Ass

See also donkey, mule.

A dull ass near home needs no spur. (8)

A thistle is a fat salad for an ass's mouth.

An ass endures his burden, but not more than his burden.

An ass is but an ass, though laden with gold.

An ass is known by his ears. (15)

An ass is the gravest beast, an owl the gravest bird. (8)

An ass laden with gold overtakes everything. (8)

An ass loaded with gold climbs to the top of a/the castle.

An ass must be tied where the master will have him.

An ass pricked must needs trot.

Asses die and wolves bury them. (8)

Asses that bray most eat least./The ass that brays most eats least.

Better (ride on) an ass that carries me/you than a horse that throws me/you.

Better be the head of an ass than the tail of a horse.

(Even) if an ass goes travelling he'll not come home a horse.

Every ass likes/loves to hear himself bray.

Every ass thinks himself worthy to stand with the king's horses.

Hay is more acceptable to an ass than gold. (Latin)

He is an ass that brays against another ass.

He that makes himself an ass, must not take it ill if men ride him. (8)

It's better to keep a cow than an ass. (9)

Jest with an ass, and he will flap you in the face with his tail. (8)

No wise man stands behind an ass when he kicks. (11)

One ass scrubs another.

Put an ass to grass and he will come home an ass. (18)

Ride a horse and mare on the shoulders, an ass and mule on the buttocks.

The ass brays when he pleases. (8)

The ass knows well in whose face he brays. (15)

The ass loaded with gold still eats thistles.

The ass that carrieth wine drinketh water. (8)

The ass that is common property is always the worst saddled. (11)

The braying of an ass does not reach heaven. (15)

The horses of hope gallop, but the asses of experience go slowly. (Russian) (11)

To a rude ass a rude keeper. (8)

What would you expect from an ass but a kick? (18)

When all men say you are an ass, it is time to bray.

When an ass kicks you, never tell it. (4)

When you hear the asses bray, we shall have rain on that day. (11)

Wherever an ass falls, there will he never fall again.

Badger

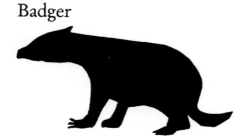

If the badger leave his hole the tod [fox] will creep in. (10)

Bear

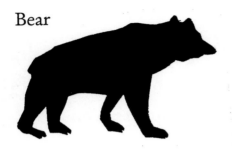

A field held in common is always ravaged by bears. (Russian) (11)

Catch your bear before you sell its skin. (16)

He must have iron nails that scratches a/with a bear./He must have iron nails that would scratch a bear.

He who shares honey with the bear has the least part of it.

Honey is too good for a bear. (8)

Little bears have all their troubles to come. (11)

One thing thinks the bear, and another he that leads him. (15)

The bear wants a tail, and cannot be a lion. (15)

The old bear falls into the old trap. (Russian) (11)

Bee

A bee never was caught in a shower. (13)

A dead bee makes no honey.

A still bee gathers no honey. (13)

A swarm of bees in May is worth a load of hay, a swarm of bees in June is worth a silver spoon, but a swarm in July is not worth a fly.

Bees that have honey in their mouths have stings in their tails.

Bees will not swarm before a near storm. (11)

Every bee's honey is sweet.

He that has sheep, swine, and bees, sleep he, wake he, he may thrive.

Honey is sweet, but the bee stings.

If bees swarm in May, they are worth a pound next day: if they swarm in July, they're not worth a fly.

If the bees stay at home, rain will come soon, if they fly away, then fine is the day. (11)

No bees, no honey; no work, no money. (4)

Old bees yield no honey./When bees are old they yield no honey.

The bee sucks honey out of the bitterest flowers.

The calf, the goose, the bee: the world is ruled by these three. (i.e. Parchment, pen and wax). (1)

What is not good for the swarm is not good for bees. (French) (11)

Where bees are, there is honey.

Where the bee sucks honey, the spider sucks poison.

Beetle

One beetle knows another. (18)/One beetle recognises another.

Every beetle is a gazelle in the eyes of its mother. (11)

Bird

See also bittern, blackbird, chicken, cock, crane, crow, cuckoo, dove, duck, eagle, fowl, gander, goose, goshawk, gosling, gull, hawk, hen, jackdaw, jay, kite, lapwing, lark, martin, nightingale, owl, partridge, peacock, pheasant, pigeon, plover, pullet, raven, robin, rook, snipe, sparrow, swallow, swan, thrush, turkey, woodcock, woodlark, wren.

A bird in the hand is worth two in a/the bush.

A bird is known by its note, and a man by his talk./The bird is known by his note, the man by his words.

A closed fist never caught a bird. (18)

A feather in hand is better than a bird in the air.

A little bird is content with a little nest./A little bird wants but a little nest.

A little string will tie a little bird. (8)

Birds are entangled by their feet, and men by their tongues.

Birds in their little nests agree.

Birds of a feather (will) flock together.

Birds once snared fear all bushes.

Destroy the nests and the birds will fly away.

Every bird as it is reared and the lark for the bog. (7)

Every bird is known by its feathers. (8)

Every bird likes its own nest best./The bird loves her nest.

Every bird loves to hear himself sing.

Every bird must hatch his/its own egg(s).

Fine feathers make fine birds.

Forbear not sowing because of birds.

He is in great want of a bird that will give a groat for an owl.

He who is not a bird should not build his nest over abysses. (11)

If the birds whistle in January there are frosts to come. (11)

If the partridge had the woodcock's thigh, it would be the best bird that ever did fly.

If wishes were thrushes, then beggars would eat birds.

In March the birds begin to search; in April the corn begins to fill; in May the birds begin to lay.

In vain the net is spread in the sight of any bird. (15)

It is a foolish bird that soils its own nest./It is ('Tis) an ill bird that fouls its own nest.

Little birds may pick a dead lion. (8)

Little birds that can sing and won't sing must/should be made to sing.

Little by little the bird builds her nest. (18)

March birds are best.

No bird soars too high if he soars with his own wings. (11)

One beats the bush and another catches the birds.

Small birds must have their meat. (i.e. Children must be fed.)

The bird must flighter [flatter] that flies with one wing. (12)

The early bird catches the worm./'Tis the early bird that catches the worm.

The fowler's pipe sounds sweet till the bird is caught. (8)

The more the bird caught in lime strives, the faster he sticks. (15)

The noisy fowler catches no birds. (8)

The older the bird the more unwillingly it parts from its feathers. (4)

The rough net is not the best catcher of birds.

The wise bird flies lowest. (18)

There are no birds in last year's nest./There are no birds of this year in last year's nests.

To fright/scare a bird is not the way to catch her/it. [frighten]

You may gape long enough ere a bird fly in your mouth.

Bitch

See also cur, dog, greyhound, hound, mastiff, pup, spaniel, whelp.

Every dog has its day, a bitch twa [two] afternoons. (9)

If the dog bark, go in; if the bitch bark, go out.

It is an ill-bred dog that will beat a bitch.

The hasty bitch brings forth blind whelps.

Bittern

A bittern makes no good hawk. (8)

Blackbird

When the blackbird sings before Christmas she will cry at Candlemas. (11)

Blindworm

If the adder could hear and the blindworm could see neither man nor beast would ever go free.

Boar

The rage of a wild boar is able to spoil more than one wood. (15)

Bream

He that has breams in his pond, is able to bid his friend welcome. (15)

Bull

See also calf, cattle, cow, heifer, ox.

He may tine [lose] a stot [young bull] that canna count his kine (10)

He that will have his farm full, must keep an old cock and a young bull.

He that would have his fold full, must keep an old tup and a young bull. (8)

In time the savage bull does bear the yoke. (15)

The bull must be taken by the horns. (16)

You may play with a bull till you get his horn in your eye.

Butterfly

Take not a musket to kill a butterfly.

Calf

See also bull, cattle, cow, heifer, ox.

A bellowing cow soon forgets her calf.

A gude [good] calf is better than a calf o' a gude kind.

An ill cow may hae [have] a gude calf.

Calf love, half love; old love, cold love.

If thou suffer a calf to be laid on thee, within a little they'll clap on the cow. (i.e. Encroachments can grow.)

Like cow, like calf. (15)

Many a good cow has a bad/an evil calf.

The calf, the goose, the bee: the world is ruled by these three. (i.e. By parchment, quill pen and wax.)

The greatest calf is not the sweetest veal.

The old cow thinks she was never a calf. (4)

They think a calf a muckle [large] beast that never saw a cow.

Camel

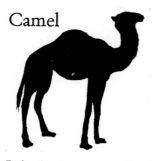

It is the last straw that breaks the camel's back./The last straw breaks the camel's back.

Men strain gnats and swallow camels. (16)

The camel, going to seek horns lost his ears.

The mair [more] the camel is bowed down, the better it serveth. (9)

Cat

See also kitten.

A baited cat may grow as fierce as a lion.

A blate [shy] cat makes a proud mouse.

A cat has nine lives.   .

A cat in gloves catches no mice.

A cat may look at a king.

A cat pent up becomes a lion. (Italian) (11)

A gloved cat was never a good hunter. (4)

A muffled cat is no good mouser.

A scalded cat fears hot water. (4)/Scalded cats fear even cold water. (8)

A winking cat's no aye [not always] blind. (10)/Though the cat winks a while, yet sure she is not blind. (8)

A wise cat never burned herself. (18)

All cats are grey in the dark.

An old cat laps as much milk as a young (kitten).

An old cat sports not with her prey.

An old cat will not burn himself. (7)

By scratching and biting, cats and dogs come together.

Can a mouse fall in love with a cat? (8)

Care killed a/the cat./Care will kill a cat.

Cast a cat ower [over] the house and she'll fa' [fall] on her feet. (10)

Cat will after kind.

Cats eat what hussies [housewives] spare./What the good wife spares, the cat eats.

Cats hide their claws.

Cats like man are flatterers. (French) (11)

Curiosity killed the cat.

Don't buy butter for cats to lick. (18)

Don't make yourself a mouse, or the cat will eat you. (16)

He hath a good hold of the cat that holds him by the skin. (8)

He that keeps the cat's dish keeps her aye [always] crying.

He that puts the cat in the pock [sack] kens [knows] best how to tak [take] her out.

He who lives with cats will get a taste for mice. (4)

How can the cat help it, if the maid be a fool?

If the cat had a churn her paw would often be in it. (7)/If the cat was churning it is often she would have her paws in it. (18)

If the cat sits long enough at the hole she will catch the mouse. (18)

It is a bold/wily mouse that breeds/nestles in the cat's ear.

It was never for nothing that the cat licked the stone.

It's for her own good that the cat purrs.

Keep no more cats than will catch mice.

Learn [teach] the cat (the road) to the kirn [churn], and she'll aye [always] be licking.

Let the cat wink, and let the mouse run.

Little by little as the cat ate the flickle [flitch]. (1)

Loud cheeps the mouse when the cat's no rustling.

Never was cat or dog drowned that could but see the shore.

One jump in the fire never burnt the cat. (18)

Put an old cat to an old rat.

Send not a cat for lard.

That cat is out of kind that sweet milk will no [not] lap.

That which comes of a cat will catch mice. (11)

The cat and the dog may kiss, yet are none the better friends.

The cat is hungry when a crust contents her.

The cat knows whose beard/lips she licks./Well knows the cat whose ear she licks. (11)

The cat shuts its eyes while it steals cream.

The cat would eat fish and/but would not wet her feet.

The cats that drive the mice away are as good as they that catch them. (German) (11)

The lickorish [lustful] cat gets many a rap.

The more you rub a cat on the rump, the higher she sets her tail. (15)

The mouse lordships where a cat is not. (8)

They that board wi' cats may count upon scarts [scratches].

To a good rat, a good cat. (11)

Too many cats are worse than rats. (18)

Two cats and a mouse, two wives in one house, two dogs and a bone, never agree in one.

Wanton kittens (may) make sober cats.

Well kens [knows] the mouse when the cat's out of the house.

What would a young cat do but eat mice/kill a mouse. (Irish)

When candles be out all cats be grey. (8)

When the cat is out the mouse can dance.

When the cat is/cat's away the mice may/will play./While the cat's away, the mice can play.

When the cat winks, little wots the mouse what the cat thinks.

When the weasel and the cat make a marriage, it is a very ill presage.

You can have no more of a cat than her/the skin.

Cattle

See also bull, calf, cow, heifer, ox.

Old cattle breed not.

Chick

See also raven.

To the raven her own chick is white./The raven thinks its own chick white/dear.

Chick(en)

See also cock, fowl, hen, pullet.

Curses, like chickens, come home to roost.

Don't count your chickens before they are hatched.

It is a poor hen that can't scrat [scratch] for one chick. (15)

Like hen, like chicken. (15)

May chickens come cheeping. (i.e. Cry feebly.)

Pick up the hen and you can gather all the chicks. (Ashanti) (11)

Though the fox run, the chicken has wings.

Where chickens feather, foxes will gather. (8)

You can't hatch chickens from fried eggs. (Dutch) (11)

Chub

Said the chevin [chub] to the trout, "My head's worth all thy bonk [body]". (8)

Cock

See also chicken, fowl, hen, pullet.

A barley-corn is better than a diamond to a cock. (8)

A cock is bold on his own dunghill.

A dead cock never crew. (18)

A fat hen makes a lean cock. (9)

A servant and a cock must/should be kept but a year.

As the cock crows, the young bird chirrups. (7)/As the old cock crows, so crows the young.

As the old cock crows, the young cock/one learns.

Every cock crows on his own dunghill.

Every cock is proud on his own dunghill.

He that will have his farm full, must keep an old cock and a young bull.

He who will have a full flock must have an old stag [gander] and a young cock./If you want to keep up the stock keep an old gander and a young cock. (18)

If the cock crows on going/goes crowing to bed, he's sure to rise with a watery head.

If the cock moult before the hen, we shall have weather thick and thin; but if the hen moult before the cock, we shall have weather (as) hard as a block.

It is a sad house where the hen crows louder than the cock.

It will be a forward cock that crows in the shell.

Let ilka [every] cock fight his ain [own] battle. (10)

"Quietness is best," as the fox said when he bit the cock's head off. (15)

The cock crows and the hen goes. (8)

The cocks crow but the hens deliver the goods. (18)

There's many a good cock come out of a tattered bag.

When the hen goes to the cock the birds (her chicks) may get a knock.

Who eats his cock alone, must saddle his horse alone.

Young cocks love no coops.

Colt

See also filly, foal, horse, jade, mare, stallion, steed.

A ragged colt may make a good horse./Many a shabby colt makes a fine horse. (7)

A wild colt may become a sober horse. (11)

Little journeys and good colt bring safe home. (8)

The best colt needs breaking. (8)

The kick of the mare hurts not the colt.

The trick the colt gets at his breaking, will, whilst he lives, ne'er be lacking. (8)

When you ride a young colt see your saddle (will) be well girt.

Young colts will canter.

Cow

See also bull, calf, cattle, heifer, ox.

A bad cow is better than none. (18)

A bellowing cow soon forgets her calf.

A horse on a cliff or a cow in a swamp, two in danger. (7)

A red cow gives good milk.

A soft-dropping April brings milk to cows and sheep. (7)

A starved cow never fills the pail. (18)

An ill (bad) cow may have a good calf.

An ill-willy [ill-natured] cow should have short horns.

Better a good cow than a cow of a good kind. (17)

Bring a cow to the hall and she'll run to the byre.

Everyone is nice till the cow gets into the garden. (18)

Faraway cows have long horns. (7)

Go to law for a sheep and lose your cow. (4)

God gives the cow, but not by the horn. (15)

God sends the shrewd cow short horns. (8)

He may tine [lose] a stot [young bull] that canna count his kine [cows]. (10)

He that aughts [owns] the cow gangs [goes] nearest her/the tail.

He that has a cow in the mire, will first put his foot in't.

He tint [lost] never a cow that grat [wept] for a needle.

I ken by my cog [milking pail] when my cow's milket [milked]. (9)

I ken by my cog [milking pail] who milks my cow. (12)

If thou suffer a calf to be laid on thee, within a little they'll clap on the cow. (i.e. Encroachments can grow.)

If you buy the cow, take the tail into the bargain.

If you sell the cow, you sell her milk too.

It's better to keep a cow than an ass. (9)

It's by the mouth o' the cow that the milk comes. (i.e. By feeding her well.) (10)

Let him that owns the cow take her by the tail. (8)

Like cow, like calf. (15)

Many a good cow has a bad/an evil calf.

Milk the cow that standeth still. (11)

Now I have a cow and a horse and everyone bids me Good morrow.

Now I have a sheep and a cow and everyone bids me "Good morrow".

Often a cow does not take after its breed. (Irish)

Take a man by his word and a cow by her horn.

The cow knows not what her tail is worth till she has lost it.

The cow little giveth that hardly liveth. (15)

The cow may die ere the grass grow.

The cow may want her tail yet. (i.e. Kindness is expected to be returned.)

The cow that's first up, gets the first of the dew.

The devil's cow calves twice a year. (15)

The old cow thinks she was never a calf. (4)

There's little value in the single cow. (7)

They think a calf a muckle [large] beast that never saw a cow.

Three things (are) not to be trusted: a cow's horn, a dog's tooth and a horse's hoof.

What is the use of a good cow when she spills her milk? (18)

When a cow tries to scratch its ear, it means a shower be very near, when it begins to thump its rib with its tail, look out for thunder, lightning and hail. (11)

When the cow is in the clout, she's soon out. (i.e. Money from her sale will be soon spent.)

When the cuckoo comes to the bare thorn, sell your cow and buy your corn; but when she comes to the full bit, sell your corn and buy your sheep.

Why buy a cow when milk is (so) cheap?

Crab

The greatest crabs be not all the best meat.

You cannot make a crab walk straight.

Crane

A wren in the hand is better than a crane to be caught. (7)

As sore fight wrens as cranes.

Crow

A carrion crow never brings luck. (English) (11)

A crow won't caw without a cause. (18)

Carrion crows bewail the dead sheep, and then eat them.

Crows are never the whiter for washing themselves.

Crows will not pick out crows' eyes./One crow never pulls out another's eyes.

Ding [knock] down the nests, and the craws [crows] will flee awa' [fly away] (9)

Every craw [crow] thinks his ain [own] bird whitest./The crow thinks her own bird(s) fairest (i.e. whitest).

Every man thinks his ain [own] craw [crow] blackest. (10)

It is ill killing a crow with an empty sling. (8)

It's God that feeds the crows that neither till, harrow, nor sow.

No carrion will kill a crow.

On the first of March, the crows begin to search.

One for the mouse, one for the crow, one to rot, and one to grow.

Pigeons are taken when crows fly at pleasure. (8)

The crow went travelling abroad and came home just as black. (11)

The fox praiseth the meat out of the crow's mouth.

The hoarse crow croaks before the rain. (15)

"They're a bonny pair," as the craw [crow] said o' his legs.

When the crow flees/flies, her tail follows.

Cub

See also tiger

Unless you enter the tiger's den, you cannot take the cubs. (Japanese) (11)

Cuckoo

Cuckoo song, is summer song. (English) (11)

In April the cuckoo shows his bill; in May, he sings all day; in June, he alters his tune; in July, away he'll fly; in August, away he must. (8)

On the third of April comes in the cuckoo and nightingale.

The cuckoo comes in April, and stays the month of May; sings a song at midsummer, and then goes away./The cuckoo comes in April, sings a song in May; then in June another tune, and then she flies away. (1)

The cuckoo has but one song. (15)

The first cock of hay frights [frightens] the cuckoo away.

The nightingale and cuckoo sing both in one month.

Turn the money [in your pocket] when you hear the cuckoo, and you'll never be without it during the year. (1)

When the cuckoo comes she eats up all the dirt. (i.e. The mire will dry up.) (1)

When the cuckoo comes to the bare thorn, sell your cow and buy your corn; but when she comes to the full bit, sell your corn and buy your sheep.

Where you hear the first call of the cuckoo, there will you be found for most of the year. (11)

Cur

See also bitch, dog, greyhound, hound, mastiff, pup, spaniel, whelp.

A cumbersome cur is hated in company.

A cur will bite before he bark.

Brabbling [wrangling] curs never want sore ears.

Yelping curs may anger mastiffs at last./Yelping curs will raise mastiffs.

You cannot trust a cur. (18)

Dam

See also colt, kid, lamb.

Every lamb knows its own dam. (8)

The kick of the dam hurts not the colt.

The litter is like to the sire and the dam. (15)

Where the dam leaps over, the kid follows.

Deer

It is not every day Daddy kills a deer. (14)

Often the hound that was made fun of killed the deer. (7)

The stricken deer withdraws herself to die. (15)

Those who hunt deer sometimes raise tigers. (Indian) (11)

Where the deer's slain some of her blood will lie.

Dog

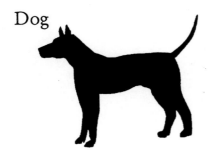

See also bitch, cur, greyhound, hound, mastiff, pup, spaniel, whelp.

A bad dog never sees the wolf.

A blind dog won't bark at the moon. (7)

A dead dog will not bark./Dead dogs bark not.

A dog does not always bark at the front gate. (Spanish) (11)

A dog is made fat in two meals.

A dog that will fetch a bone will carry a bone./The dog that fetches will carry. (i.e. An unworthy person will pass on secrets.)

A dog will bark before he bite./Dogs bark before they bite.

A dog will not cry/howl if you beat him with a bone./Strike a dog with a bone and he'll not growl.

A dog with two homes is never any good. (18)

A good dog deserves a good bone.

A gude [good] dog ne'er barkit [barked] about a bane [bone]. (10)

A kennel is lodging good enough for a dog. (15)

A living dog is better than a dead lion.

A man has his hour, and a dog has his day.

A man may cause/provoke his own dog to bite him.

A man's best friend is his dog. (6)

A reasonable amount of fleas is good for dog, it keeps him from brooding. (11)

A/the scalded dog fears cold water.

A stick is quickly found to beat a dog with./It is easy to find a stick to beat a dog.

A toiling dog comes halting home. (15)

A dog does not flee from a bone. (i.e. Even though it be thrown at him.) (14)

A weel [well] bred dog gaes [goes] out when he sees them preparing to kick him out. (9)

All are not thieves that dogs bark at.

An/the old dog barks not in vain./Old dogs bark not for nothing./When the old dog barks it is time to watch. (Latin)

An old dog bites sore.

An old dog cannot alter his way of barking. (18)

An old dog will learn no new tricks./You cannot teach an old dog new tricks.

As a wolf is like a dog, so is a flatterer like a friend.

At open doors dogs come in.

Barking dogs bite not the sorest. (8)

Barking dogs seldom bite.

Beat the dog before the lion.

Better a dog fawn on you than bark at you.

Better be the head of a dog than the tail of a lion.

Better to have a dog fawn on you than bite you.

Beware of a silent dog and still water. (German) (11)

Brag is a good dog but dares not bite.

Brag is a good dog, but Holdfast is better.

By scratching and biting, cats and dogs come together.

Cut off a dog's tail and he will be a dog still.

Do not/don't keep a dog and bark yourself.

Dog does not eat dog.

Dogs and bairns are aye [always] fond of fools. (9)

Dogs are fine in the field. (15)

Dogs bark as they are bred.

Dogs begin in jest and end in earnest.

Dogs gnaw bones because they cannot swallow them.

Dogs that bark at a distance bite not at hand/never bite.

Dogs that put up many hares kill none.

Dogs wag their tails not so much in love to you as to your bread.

Dogs redd swine. (i.e. A third party will put two other parties in order.)

Dumb dogs are dangerous. (4)

Every dog has his day and some have two. (18)/Every dog has its day, a bitch twa [two] afternoons. (9)

Every dog has its duties. (18)

Every dog is a lion at home.

Every dog is allowed his first bite.

Every dog is valiant at his own door.

Fiddlers, dogs, and flies, come to feasts uncalled.

Folk's dogs bark worse than themselves. (i.e. Servants can be more intimidating than masters.)

Folly is a bonny dog.

Gie [give] a/the greedy dog a muckle bane [big bone].

Give a dog a bad name and hang him./Give a dog a bad name and it will hang him. (11)

Good jests bite like lambs, not like dogs. (8)

He that has nothing to spare must not keep a dog./Who has no more bread than need, must not keep a dog.

He that keeps another man's dog shall have nothing left him but the line.

He that strikes my dog would strike me if he durst [dared].

He who lies (down) with dogs will rise with fleas./If you lie down with dogs you'll rise with fleas./Who lies with dogs shall rise up with fleas. (Latin)

Hold on to the bone and the dog will follow you./Keep hold of the bone and the dog will follow you./Keep the bone and the dog will follow.

Hungry dogs will eat dirty puddings.

Idle dogs worry sheep.

If the dog bark, go in; if the bitch bark, go out.

If the old dog bark, he gives counsel.

If three dogs chase a rabbit they cannot kill it. (11)

If you want a pretence to whip a dog, it is enough to say he eat up the frying pan.

If you wish the dog to follow you, feed him.

In every country dogs bite.

Into the mouth of a bad dog falls many/often falls a good bone.

It is a good dog that can catch anything. (8)

It is a poor dog that is not worth (the) whistling.

It is an ill [bad] dog that deserves not a crust.

It is an ill-bred dog that will beat a bitch.

It is hard to make a bed for the dog. (15)

It is hard to make an old dog stoop low.

It is hard to put a dog off his track. (18)

It would vex a dog to see a pudding creep.

It's hard to make a choice between two blind dogs. (18)

It's hard to teach an old dog to dance. (15)

Keep a dog for your friend, and in your other hand a stick. (15)

Let sleeping dogs lie.

Little dogs have long tails.

Little dogs start the hare, the great get her.

Look not for musk in a dog's kennel.

Love me, love my dog.

Many dogs may easily worry one hare. (i.e. kill her.)

Many dogs soon eat up a horse.

Modest dogs miss much meat. (11)

Never was cat or dog drowned that could but see the shore.

Quarrelling dogs come halting home.

Quarrelsome dogs get dirty coats.

The best dogs leap the stile first.

The cat and the dog may kiss, yet are none the better friends.

The dog barks in vain at the moon. (15)

The dog bites the stone, not him that throws it.

The dog that is idle barks at his fleas, but he that is hunting feels them not.

The dog that licks ashes trust not with meal.

The dog that trots about finds a bone. (15)

The dogs bark, but the caravan goes/moves on. (Arabian)

The foremost dog catches/grips the hare.

The gude [good] dog doesna aye [always] get the best bane [bone].

The hindmost dog may catch the hare.

The lean dog is a' fleas.

The mad dog bites his master.

The silent dog is always the first to bite. (German) (11)

The moon does not heed the barking of dogs.

They're scarce o' horse flesh that rides on the dog. (9)

They're keen o' company that taks [take] the dog on their back. (10)

Three things (are) not to be trusted: a cow's horn, a dog's tooth and a horse's hoof.

Too much pudding will choke a dog.

Trust not a horse's heel, nor a dog's tooth.

Two cats and a mouse, two wives in one house, two dogs and a bone, never agree in one.

Two dogs fight/strive for a bone, and a third runs away with it./While two dogs are fighting for a bone, a third runs away with it.

"We hounds killed the hare," quoth the lap-dog. (8)

We may not expect a good whelp from an ill [bad] dog.

We will bark ourselves rather than buy dogs so dear.

When your hand is in the dog's mouth withdraw it gently. (7)

When a dog is drowning, everyone offers him drink.

When one dog barks another will join it. (Latin)

While the dog gnaws (the) bone, companions would he none.

While you trust to the dog, the wolf slips into the sheepfold.

Who gives bread to other's dogs is often barked at by his own. (Italian) (11)

You can never scare a dog away from a greasy hide. (i.e. Bad habits are difficult to overcome.) (3)

Donkey

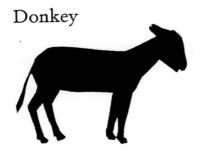

See also ass, mule.

It is/'Tis time to cock your hay and corn, when the old donkey blows his horn.

Scabby donkeys scent each other over nine hills. (4)

Send a donkey to Paris, he'll return no wiser than he went. (4)

The donkey means one thing and the driver another. (3)

Dove

See also pigeon.

Eagles do not breed doves.

Fair dovecotes have most doves. (15)

Loud coos the doo/dow [dove] when the hawk's no whistling.

Duck

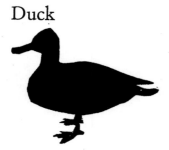

A duck will not always dabble in the same gutter.

Ducks won't lay till they've sipped March water. (13)

It's natural for ducks to go barefoot. (18)

Prate is (but) prate; but it's the duck lays the eggs/that lays the egg.

When November's ice will bear a duck, winter will be all slosh and muck. (11)

Eagle

Eagles do not breed doves.

Eagles catch no flies./The eagle does not (stoop to) catch flies.

Eagles fly alone, but sheep flock together.

Only the eagle can gaze at the sun. (15)

The ignorant have an eagle's wings and an owl's eyes.

Wrens may prey where eagles dare not perch. (8)

Eel

All that breed in the mud are not eels. (8)

He has a sliddrey grip that has an eel by the tail.

He that will catch eels must disturb the flood. (15)

It's late to be mending your nets when the eels are in the river. (18)

Mud chokes no eels.

Put your hand in the creel [fisherman's basket], tak [take] out (either) an adder or an eel.

You cannot hide an eel in a sack.

Elephant

An elephant never forgets.

Only an elephant can bear an elephant's load. (3)

Ermine

In an ermine spots are soon discovered.

Ewe

See also lamb, ram, sheep, wether.

As soon goes the young lamb's skin to the market as the old ewe's.

Many frosts and many thowes [thaws] make many rotten yowes [ewes].

Now I have got an ewe and a lamb, everyone cries, "Welcome, Peter".(8)

The ewe that doth bleat doth lose most of her meat. (8)

When a/the ewe's drowned she's dead.

Filly

See also colt, foal, horse, jade, mare, stallion, steed.

When the mare has a bald face the filly will have a blaze. (i.e. A white mark on its face.)

Fish

See also bream, chub, eel, hake, herring, mackerel, pike, salmon, sprat, sturgeon, trout.

All fish are not caught with flies.

All is/all's fish that comes to my/the net.

An ill [bad] fish gets an ill bait. (i.e. Bad people get what they deserve.)

Better are/is a small fish than an empty dish.

Big fish eat little fish.

Fish must swim (thrice).

Fresh fish and poor friends become soon ill savoured. (15)

Gut not the fish till you get them.

"I was taken by a morsel," says the fish.

If you swear, you'll catch no fish.

In a great river great fish are found: but take heed lest you be drowned.

It is a silly fish that is caught twice with the same bait.

It is in vain to cast your net when there is no fish.

It is not fish until it is on the bank. (Irish) (11)

It is rare to find a fish that will not some time or other bite./'Tis rare to find a fish that will not bite some time or other.

It's good fish when it is gripped [caught]./'Tis good fish if it were but caught.

Keep your ain [own] fish guts for your ain sea-maws [seagulls].

Little fish are/is sweet.

Little fishes slip through nets, but great fishes are taken.

Of all the fish in the sea herring is the king.

Sma' fish are better than nane [none]. (10)

That/the fish will soon be caught that nibbles at every bait.

The best fish swim(s) near the bottom.

The cat would eat fish and/but would not wet her feet.

The fish adores the bait. (8)

The fish dies by its mouth. (Portuguese) (11)

The fish may be caught in a net that will not come to the hook. (11)

The fish that's bred in a dirty puddle will aye taste o' mud.

The great fish eat up the small. (15)

The net of the sleeper catches fish.

The sea has fish for every man.

There are as good fish in the sea as ever came out of it.

There are finer fish in the sea than have ever been caught. (19)

Venture a small fish to catch a great one.

When the corn is in the shock the fish are on the rock.

When the fish is caught, the net is/nets are laid aside.

Flea

A reasonable amount of fleas is good for dog, it keeps him from brooding. (11)

Big fleas have little fleas./Great fleas have lesser fleas./Great fleas have little fleas upon their backs to bite 'em. (11)

Do nothing hastily but (the) catching of fleas./Nothing must be done hastily but killing of fleas.

He who lies with dogs rises with fleas./If you lie down with dogs you'll rise with fleas./Who lies with dogs shall rise up with fleas.(Latin)

If you kill one flea in March you kill a hundred.

The dog that is idle barks at his fleas, but he that is hunting feels them not.

The lean dog is a' fleas.

When eager bites the thirsty flea, clouds and rain you'll surely see. (11)

Where the chamber is swept and wormwood thrown, no flea for her life dare bide to be known. (13)

Fly

A closed/shut mouth catches no flies.

A fly may sting a horse and make him wince. (11)

Daub yoursel' wi' honey and ye'll ne'er want flies. (9)

Do not remove a fly from your friend's forehead with a hatchet. (11)

Don't imitate the fly before you have wings. (French) (11)

Eagles catch no flies./Eagles don't catch flies.

Fiddlers, dogs, and flies, come to feasts uncalled.

Flies go to/haunt lean horses.

Honey catches more flies than vinegar.

Hungry flies bite sore.

Into a mouth shut flies fly not.

Law catches/Laws catch flies but let hornets go free.

Make yourself all honey and the flies will devour you.

Of small account is a fly till it gets into the eye. (18)

The fly has her spleen, and the ant her gall.

The fly that plays too long in the candle, singes his wings at last.

To a boiling pot flies come not.

When harvest flies hum, there's warm weather to come. (11)

You must lose a fly to catch a trout.

Foal

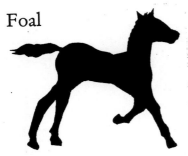

See also colt, filly, horse, jade, mare, stallion, steed.

How can the foal amble when the horse and mare trot?

It's lang [long] ere ye saddle a foal. (10)

Fowl

Fair feathers make fair fowls.

Fox

A foolish fox is caught by one leg, but a wise one by all four. (Serbian) (11)

A fox is not taken twice in the same snare. (1)

A fox should not be of the jury at a goose's trial.

A wise fox will never rob his neighbour's henroost. (French) (11)

An old fox is not easily snared.

An old fox is shy of a trap. (18)

An old fox need learn/needs no craft.

An old fox understands a/the trap.

As long as you serve the tod [fox] you must carry/bear up his tail.

As long runs the fox as he has feet.

At length the fox is brought to the furrier.

Beware the geese when the fox preaches./When the fox preaches, (then) beware/take care of your geese.

Curses make the tod [fox] fat.

Every fox must pay his own skin to the flayer./Every fox must pay his skin to the furrier/slayer. (i.e. A crafty person is finally caught.)

Fie upon hens, quoth the fox, because he could not reach them.

Foxes dig not their (own) holes.

Foxes prey farthest from their earths./The fox preys farthest from his hole/home.

He is a proud tod [fox] that will not scrape his own hole.

He that has a fox for his mate has need of a net at his girdle.

He that will deceive the fox must rise betimes./He that will get the better of a fox must rise early.

He's a dirty tod [fox] that fyles [fouls] his ain [own] hole. (9)

I care not whether the tod [fox] worry the goose or the goose worry the tod.

If the badger leave his hole the tod [fox] will creep in. (10)

If you deal with a fox, think of his tricks.

Ill herds make fat foxes.

In spite of the fox's cunning, his skin is often sold. (7)

It is a blind goose that comes to the fox's sermon.

It is an ill sign to see a fox lick a lamb.

It is good to follow the old fox. (15)

It is ill to make a blawer [blowing] horn of a tod's [fox's] tail. (12)

"More beard than brains," as the fox said of the goat. (18)

Old foxes want no tutors.

"Quietness is best", as the fox said when he bit the cock's head off. (15)

The brains of a fox will be of little service, if you play with a paw of a lion. (15)

The fox fares best when he is banned/cursed.

The fox knows much, but more he that catcheth him.

The fox is known by his brush [furred tail]. (15)

The fox may grow grey but never good.

The fox never found a better messenger than himself./The tod [fox] never sped better than when he went his own errand.

The fox praiseth the meat out of the crow's mouth.

The fox that had lost its tail would persuade others out of theirs.

The fox's wiles will never enter the lion's head./The wiles of the fox will never enter the lion's head.

The sleepy fox has seldom feathered breakfast.

The tail does often catch the fox.

The tod [fox] keeps aye [always] his own hole clean.

The tod's [fox's] bairns/whelps are ill to tame.

There's mony [many] a tod [fox] hunted that's no killed. (10)

Though the fox run, the chicken has wings.

We can have no more of the fox but the skin./You can have no more of a fox than the skin.

When the fox has once got in his nose, he'll soon find means to make his body follow. (15)

When the tod [fox] gets to the wood he cares not who keek [peep] in his tail. (i.e. An escaped villain will look after himself.)

When the tod [fox] preaches tak [take] care o' the lambs.

When the tod preiches [preaches] bewar [beware] of the hens. (4)

Where chickens feather, foxes will gather. (8)

Frog

An April flood carries away the frog and her brood.

Every little frog is great in his own bog. (18)

Gossips are frogs, they drink and talk.

He is a fond fisher that angles for a frog. (15)

If the frog and the mouse quarrel, the kite will see them agreed.

The frog cannot out of her bog.

The frog said to the harrow, "Cursed be so many lords".

We have fished fair and caught a frog. (8)

You can't pluck a frog. (18)

Gander

See also goose, gosling.

As deep drinks the goose as the gander.

As the gander, so is the goose. (8)

Goose and gander and gosling are three sounds, but one thing.

He who will have a full flock must have an old stag [gander] and a young cock./If you want to keep up the stock keep an old gander and a young cock.

Sauce for the goose is sauce for the gander./What is sauce for the goose is sauce for the gander.

The beak of the goose is no longer than that of the gander. (7)

There is no goose so grey in the lake that cannot find a gander for her make [mate]. (15)

Glow-worm

When the glow-worm lights her lamp, the air is always (very) damp.

Gnat

Men strain at gnats and swallow camels. (16)

Goat

See also kid.

An old goat is never the more reverend [revered] for his beard.

Do not mistake a goat's beard for a fine stallion's tail.[*]

Goats are not sold at every fair. (8)

If the beard were all, the goat might preach.

If you put a silk dress on a goat he is a goat still./If you put a silk suit on a goat it is still a goat.

It is difficult to cut wool off a goat. (18)

It's difficult to choose between two blind goats.

"More beard than brains," as the fox said of the goat. (18)

The goat gives a good milking, but she casts it all down with her foot.

The goat must bleat where he/she is tied.

The goat must browse where she is tied.

[*] *Irish Proverbs*, Appletree Press

Goose

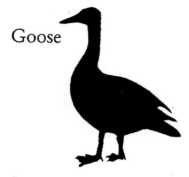

See also gander, gosling.

A gude [good] goose may hae [have] an ill [bad] gaislin [gosling] (10)

A wild goose never laid a tame egg/tame eggs./A wild goose never lays a tame egg.

A wild goose never reared a tame gosling.*

As deep drinks the goose as the gander.

As the gander, so is the goose. (8)

Beware the geese when the fox preaches./When the fox preaches, beware/take care of the/your geese.   –

By little and little the wolf eats (up) the goose.

Don't pluck your goose until you catch her. (18)

Feather by feather the goose can be/is plucked.

Gane [gone] is the goose that laid the muckle [great] egg./Gone is the goose that the great egg did lay.

Goose and gander and gosling are three sounds, but one thing.

Goslings lead the geese to grass/water.

He that eats of the king's goose shall be choked with feathers. (11)

---

* *Irish Proverbs*, Appletree Press

He that has a goose will get a goose.

I care not whether the tod worry the goose or the goose worry the tod [fox].

If all fools wore feathers/white caps we should seem a flock of geese.

If I canna [cannot] keep geese I can keep gaislins [goslings]. (i.e. Revenge is taken on the injurer's dependants.)

It is a blind goose that knows not a fox from a fern bush. (8)

It is a silly goose that comes to a/the fox's sermon.

It's ill [bad] taking corn frae [from] geese.

Kill not the goose that lays the golden egg(s).

On Valentine's Day will a good goose lay; if she be a good goose, her dame well to pay, she will lay two eggs before Valentine'sDay.

Sauce for the goose is sauce for the gander./What is sauce for the goose is sauce for the gander.

The beak of the goose is no longer than that of the gander. (7)

The calf, the goose, the bee: the world is ruled by these three. (i.e. By parchment, quill pen and wax.)

The three most fortunate things a man ever had; a mare, a sow and a goose. (7)

There is no goose so grey in the lake that cannot find a gander for her make [mate] (15)

Water for the goose and alms for the beggar. (7)

When the rain rains and the goose winks, little wots the gosling what the goose thinks.

When you're ser'd [served] the geese are watered.

Wherever there are women there's talking, and wherever there's geese there's cackling. (7)

Goshawk

A goshawk beats not a bunting.

Gosling

See also gander, goose.

A gude [good] goose may hae [have] an ill [bad] gaislin [gosling].

A wild goose never reared a tame gosling.[*]

Goose and gander and gosling are three sounds, but one thing.

Goslings lead the geese to grass/water.

If I canna [cannot] keep geese I can keep gaislins [goslings]. (i.e. Revenge is taken on the injurer's dependants.)

When the rain rains and the goose winks, little wots the gosling what the goose thinks.

---

[*] *Irish Proverbs*, Appletree Press

Greyhound

See also bitch, cur, dog, hound, mastiff, pup, spaniel, whelp.

A greyhound finds its food in its feet. (Irish)

It is natural to a greyhound to have a long tail. (8)

Gull (Seagull)

If the gulls are out, good luck's about. (11)

Keep your own fish-guts for your own sea-maws [seagulls].

No gulls, no luck. (French) (11)

The gull comes after the rain. (8)

The gull comes against the rain.

Hake

Often a man cast a sprat to catch a hake. (Irish)

What we lose in hake we shall have in herring.

Hare

A blind man may sometimes catch the hare. (15)

By chance a cripple may grip a hare.

Drumming is not the way to catch a hare. (8)

Even a hare will insult a dead lion. (Latin)

First catch your hare.

Hares can gambol over the body of a dead lion. (11)

Hares may pull dead lions by the beard.

If you run after two hares, you will catch neither./He who hunts two hares leaves one and loses the other. (3)

Little dogs start the hare, the great get her.

Long runs the hare but she is caught at last. (18)

Many dogs may easily worry one hare. (i.e. Kill.)

Nearly never killed the hare. (18)

The foremost dog catches/grips the hare.

The hare always returns to her form. (4)

The hare starts when a man least expects it.

The hindmost dog may catch the hare.

The tortoise wins the race while the hare is sleeping.

'Tis hard to drive a hare out of a bush he's not in.

"Up and at it again," as the hedgehog said to the hare. (18)

"We hounds killed the hare," quoth the lap-dog.

You cannot run with the hare and hunt with the hounds.

Hawk

See also goshawk.

A bittern makes no good hawk. (8)

A carrion kite will never be a good hawk.

A closed hand catches no hawk./A shut fist will not catch a hawk.

Empty hands no hawks allure./With empty hands men may no hawks allure.

Hawks will not pick out hawks' eyes.

Highflying hawks are fit for princes.

Loud coos the doo/dow [dove] when the hawk's no whistling.

Pheasants are fools if they invite the hawk to dinner. (8)

The haughty hawk winna [will not] stoop to carrion.

There's nae [no] hawk flees [flies]/soars sae [so] high but will stoop to some lure.

Hedgehog

Hedgehogs lodge among thorns, because they themselves are prickly.

"Up and at it again," as the hedgehog said to the hare. (18)

Heifer

See also bull, calf, cattle, cow, ox.

Quey [heifer] calves are dear veal.

Hen

See also chicken, cock, fowl, pullet.

A/the black hen lays a white egg/white eggs.

A fat hen makes a lean cock. (9)

A hen that lays without, has need of a white nest-egg.

A layin' hen is better than a standin' mill.

A laying hen is better than a nest of eggs. (18)

Better an egg today than a hen tomorrow.

Fat hens are aye [always] ill layers./Fat hens lay few eggs. (German)

"Fie upon hens," quoth the fox, because he could not reach them.

Grain by grain the hen fills her belly. (8)

He that comes of a hen must scrape.

He that would have eggs must endure the cackling of hens./If you will have the hen's egg, you must bear her cackling.

If a/the hen does not prate, she will not lay./If a hen does not prate she'll never lay.

If the cock moult before the hen, we shall have weather thick and thin; but if the hen moult before the cock, we shall have weather (as) hard as a block.

It is a poor hen that can't scrat [scratch] for one chick. (15)

It is a sad house where the hen crows louder than the cock.

It is better to have a hen tomorrow than an egg today. (8)

It is no good hen that cackles in your house and lays in another's. (15)

It is not the hen that cackles most lays the largest egg.

It's a bad hen that won't scratch herself./It is a bad hen can't scrape for herself.

It's only a worthless hen that fails to provide for herself. (7)

Like hen, like chicken. (15)

Never offer your hen for sale on a rainy day.

Pick up the hen and you can gather all the chicks. (Ashanti) (11)

The cock crows and the hen goes. (8)

The cocks crow but the hens deliver the goods.

The sitting hen never fattens. (18)

Though the hen may lay out her eggs will be found. (18)

When the hen goes to the cock the birds [her chicks] may get a knock.

When the tod [fox] preiches [preaches] bewar [beware] of the hens. (4)

You can't expect a big egg from a little hen. (18)

Herring

A herring in the pan is worth twenty in the sea. (18)

Every herring must hang by its own gill./Let every herring hing [hang] by its own head/tail.

Of all the fish in the sea herring is the king.

Seven herrings are a meal for a salmon. (18)

What we lose in hake we shall have in herring.

Hog

See also pig, sow, swine.

A hog on trust grunts till he's paid. (11)

A hog that's bemired endeavours to bemire others.

Better my hog dirty home than no hog at all.

Draff [hogwash] is good enough for hogs.

Every hog his own apple.

He who does not kill hogs, will not get black puddings.

It is hard to break a hog of an ill custom.

It is ill [unwise] to drive black hogs in the dark.

The hog never looks up to him that threshes down the acorns.

The worst hog often gets the best pear.

What can you expect from a hog but a grunt?

Hornet

Law catches/Laws catch flies but let hornets go free.

Horse

See also colt, filly, foal, jade, mare, stallion, steed.

A boisterous horse must have a rough bridle.

A cough will stick longer by a horse than a peck of oats. (11)

A dapple-grey horse will sooner die than tire. (11)

A flea-bitten horse never tires. (15)

A full [drunk] man and a hungry horse mak [make] good speed home.

A gentle/good horse should be seldom spurred.

A good horse cannot be of a bad colour./Good horses can't be of a bad colour.

A good horse oft needs a good spur. (15)

A grey horse looks well in a bog. (18)

A hired horse is a tired horse never./A hired horse tired never.

A horse is neither better nor worse for his trappings. (8)

A horse may stumble that has four legs.

A horse on a cliff or a cow in a swamp, two in danger. (7)

A horse that will not carry a saddle must have no oats.

A hungry horse makes a clean manger./Hungry horses make a clean manger.

A jade eats as much as a good horse.

A kindly aver [natural work-horse] will never make a good horse.

A man/you may lead a horse to (the) water, but he/you cannot make him drink.

A man without religion is like a horse without a bridle. (15)

A mare's shoe and a horse's shoe are both alike.

A nod is as good as a wink to a blind horse.

A pair of spurs to a borrowed horse is better than a peck of oats. (11)

A ragged colt may make a good horse./Many a shabby colt makes a fine horse. (7)

A running horse is an open grave.

A scald [scabby] horse is good enough for a scabbed squire. (i.e. Mean things become mean people.)

A short horse is soon curried.

A spur and a whip for a dull horse. (15)

A wild colt may become a sober horse. (11)

A young trooper should have an old horse. (8)

Ae [one] man may take a horse to the water, but twenty winna gar [will not make] him drink.

All lay (the) load on a/the willing horse./Everyone lays a burden on the willing horse.

An eating horse ne'er founder'd.

An inch of a nag [riding-horse] is worth a span of an aver [work-horse].

An old horse needs fresh grass. (18)

Beggars mounted run their horses to death. (11)

Better a lean horse than an empty halter.

Better (ride on) an ass that carries you than a horse that throws you.

Better be the head of an ass than the tail of a horse.

Do not spur a free horse.

Do not swap horses when crossing a stream. (15)/Don't change horses in midstream.

Don't judge a horse by the harness. (11)

Don't refuse to sell your horse for the sake of a crown. (7)

Don't ride the high horse.

Don't put the cart before the horse. (16)

Don't shut the stable-door after the horse has bolted./It is too late to shut the stable-door after the horse has bolted.

Either win the horse or lose the saddle.

Even a good horse cannot keep running. (Irish)

Every horse thinks his/its own pack heaviest.

Flies go to/haunt lean horses.

For want of a nail the shoe is/was lost; for want of a shoe the horse is/was lost; for want of a horse the rider is/was lost.

Forgive a horse that will cock his ears. (7)

Furniture and mane make the horse sell. (8)

Gamesters and racehorses never last long.

Good horses make short miles. (15)

Hang not all your bells upon one horse. (8)

Happiness is not a horse, you cannot harness it. (Russian) (11)

Have a horse of your own and you may borrow another/another's.

He is a gentle horse that never cast his rider.

He is free of a horse that never had one.

He that hires the horse must ride before.

He's a good horse that pulls his own load. (18)

He's a proud horse that will not bear his own corn.

He's a weak horse that dow not [is not able to] bear the saddle. (12)

He's an auld [old] horse that winna nicher [will not neigh] when he sees corn. (10)

He's/'Tis an ill horse that can neither whinny nor wag his tail.

Hounds and horses devour their masters.

How can the foal amble when the horse and mare trot?

If two men ride (on) a horse, one must ride behind.

If wishes were horses, beggars would ride.

If you can't ride two horses at once, you shouldn't be in a circus.

In a frost a nail is worth a/the horse. (i.e. The nail could save the horse from falling.)

In selling a horse praise his bad points, and leave the good ones to look after themselves. (11)

It is a good horse that never stumbles, and a good wife that never grumbles.

It is a proud horse that will not bear his own provender.

It is easy to drive with your own whip and another's horse. (18)

It is not the day you are harrowing you should feed your horse.

It is the bridle and spur that makes a good horse.

It is too late to lock/shut the stable-door when the horse is stolen. (15)

It is useless to flog a dead horse. (16)

Lay/set the saddle upon the right horse./Put/set the saddle on the right horse.

Lend your horse for a long journey, you may have him return with his skin.

Let a horse drink when he will, not what he will.

Let the muckle [big] horse get the muckle windlin [burden].

Let the best horse leap the hedge first. (8)

Light lades [loads] mak [make] willing horses.

Little may an old horse do, that may not nigher [neigh].

Many dogs soon eat up a horse.

Mettle is dangerous in a blind horse.

Money makes the horse gallop whether he has shoes or not. (18)

Never look a gift [given] horse in the mouth./Don't look a gift horse in the mouth.

Never spur a willing horse.

Now I have a cow and a horse and everyone bids me Good morrow.

One cannot shoe a running horse. (Dutch) (11)

One horse scrubs another.

One saddle is enough for one horse. (11)

One thing thinks the horse, and another he that rides/saddles him./The horse thinks one thing, and he that saddles him another.

Pride's an ill horse to ride. (10)

Ride a horse and mare on the shoulders, an ass and mule on the buttocks.

Rub a galled [scabbed] horse on the back and he will wince./Touch a galled horse (on the back) and he'll kick/wince.

The best horse doesn't always win the race. (18)

The best horse jumps the ditch. (18)

The best horse needs breaking, and the aptest child needs teaching.

The biggest horses are not the best travellers.

The blind horse is the hardiest.

The borrowed horse has hard hoofs. (7)

The common horse is worst shod. (1)

The fault of the horse is put on the saddle. (8)

The grey mare is the better horse. (i.e. the wife.)

The horse next to the mill carries all the grist.

The horse that draws after him his halter is not altogether escaped.

The horse that has been struck on the head is timid thereafter. (14)

The horses of hope gallop, but the asses of experience go slowly. (Russian) (11)

The losing horse blames the saddle. (7)

The master's eye makes the horse fat.

The old horse may die waiting for the new grass.

The slow horse reaches the mill. (7)

The stable wears out a horse more than the road. (French) (11)

The stout horse gets aye [always] the hard wark [work]. (9)

The strongest horse loups [jumps] the dike.

The willing horse is aye [always] worked to death. (10)

There is life in the old horse yet. (15)

They are good willie [generous] of their horses that hes [have] nane [none]. (4)

They're scarce [scared] o' horse flesh that rides [ride] on the dog. (9)

Those who would slight my horse would buy my horse. (18)

Three things (are) not to be trusted: a cow's horn, a dog's tooth and a horse's hoof.

To a greedy eating horse a short halter. (15)

Toom [empty] stalls make biting horses.

Trouble rides a fast horse. (Italian) (11)

Trust not a horse's heel nor a dog's tooth.

When the horse is at the gallop the bridle's ower [too] late.

Where the horse lies down there some hair will be found.

While the grass grows, the horse starves.

Who eats his cock alone, must saddle his horse alone.

Who has a good horse in his stable can go afoot. (11)

Who has no horse may ride on a staff. (15)

You can't judge a horse by his harness. (18)

You may know the horse by his/the harness.

Zeal without knowledge is a runaway horse. (4)

Hound

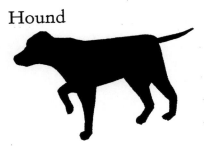

See also bitch, cur, dog, greyhound, mastiff, pup, spaniel, whelp.

At times the slow hound is lucky. (18)

Every hound is a pup till he hunts. (7)

Hounds and horses devour their masters.

Often the hound that was made fun of killed the deer. (7)

The hungry hound thinks not of her whelps. (7)

The slow hound often has good qualities./A slow-footed hound often has good qualities. (18)

"We hounds killed the hare," quoth the lap-dog.

While the hound gnaws bone, companions would he none.

You cannot run with the hare and hunt with the hounds.

Jackdaw

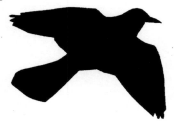

Jackdaw always perches by jackdaw. (4)

Jade

See also colt, filly, foal, horse, mare, stallion, steed.
A jade eats as much as a good horse.
Better a lean jade than an empty halter. (4)
Spur a jade a question, and he'll/she'll kick you an answer. (15)

Jay

One cherry-tree suffices not two jays.

Kid

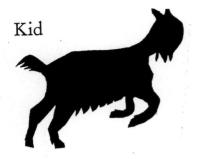

See also dam, goat.

The kid that keeps above is in no danger of the wolf.

Where the dam leaps over, the kid follows.

Kite

A carrion kite will never be a good hawk.

A leg of a lark is better than the body of a kite.

Ask a kite for a feather, and she'll say, she has but just enough to fly with.

If the frog and the mouse quarrel, the kite will see them agreed.

It was never for nothing that the gled [kite] whistled.

Kitten

See also cat.

Mice care not to play with kittens. (8)

Wanton kittens (may) make sober cats.

Ladybird

Plenty of ladybirds, plenty of hops.

Lamb

See also ewe, ram, sheep, wether.

A lamb when carried far becomes as burdensome as a sheep. (14)

A pet lamb makes a cross ram. (11)

As soon goes the young lamb's skin to the market as the old ewe's.

Death devours lambs as well as sheep.

Every lamb knows its own dam. (8)

Go to bed with the lamb, and rise with the lark.

God tempers the wind to the shorn lamb.

God's lambs will play. (i.e. Children will at times be disorderly.)

Good jests bite like lambs, not like dogs. (8)

It is an ill sign to see a fox lick a lamb.

March comes in like a lion and goes out like a lamb.

Now I have got an ewe and a lamb, every one cries, "Welcome, Peter".(8)

Pigs grow fat where lambs would starve. (11)

The lamb is a sheep in the long run. (7)

The life of the wolf is the death of the lamb. (15)

When sheep and lambs do gambol and fight, the weather will change before the night. (11)

When the tod [fox] preaches tak [take] care o' the lambs. (4)

Lapwing

The lapwing cries farthest from her nest.

Lark

A leg of a lark is better than the body of a kite.

Every bird as it is reared and the lark for the bog. (7)

Go to bed with the lamb, and rise with the lark.

I would rather hear the lark sing than the mouse cheep./It is better to hear the lark sing than the mouse cheep/chirp.

If the sky falls we shall catch larks.

Lovers live by love as larks live by leeks.

Leech

An/the empty leech sucks sore.

Leopard

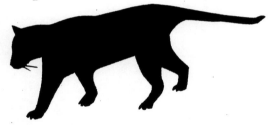

A/the leopard cannot change his spots.

In a leopard the spots are not observed.

Lion

A baited cat may grow as fierce as a lion.

A lion is not a safe companion for all persons. (7)

A lion may (come to) be beholden to a mouse.

A/the lion's skin is never cheap.

A living dog is better than a dead lion.

A man is a lion in his own cause. (i.e. A good cause.)

A mouse may help a lion.

Beat the dog before the lion.

Better be the head of a dog than the tail of a lion.

Destroy the lion while he is but/yet a whelp.

Even a hare will insult a dead lion. (Latin)

Hares can gambol over the body of a dead lion. (11)

He that has his hand in the lion's mouth must take it out as well as he can.

Hunger will conquer a lion. (18)

It is better to be [the] head of a lizard than the tail of a lion. (8)

Little birds may pick a dead lion. (8)

March comes like a lion and goes out like a lamb.

One, but that one a lion.

The bear wants a tail, and cannot be a lion. (15)

The brains of a fox will be of little service if you play with a paw of a lion. (15)

The fox's wiles will never enter the lion's head./The wiles of the fox will never enter the lion's head.

The lion is known by his claws [paws]./You can tell the lion by his paw.

The lion is not so fierce as he is painted/they paint him.

The lion spares the suppliant.

Though thy enemy seem a mouse, yet watch him like a lion.

Wake not a sleeping lion.

Who takes a lion when he is absent, fears a mouse present. (4)

Lizard

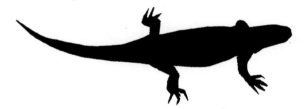

A lizard on a cushion will still seek leaves. (Russian) (11)

It is better to be [the] head of a lizard than the tail of a lion. (8)

Whom a serpent has bitten, a lizard alarms.

Louse

A beggar pays a benefit with a louse. (4)

A hungry louse bites sore.

A louse is better than no meat.

A rogue's wardrobe is harbour for a louse. (15)

Better a louse in the pot than no flesh at all.

Gie [give] a beggar a bed, and he'll pay you wi' a louse.

He that marries a beggar gets a louse for a tocher [dowry].

Lice do not bite busy men. (4)

Louse is a beggar's companion. (15)

Nits will be lice.

Nothing so crouse [brisk] as a new washen [washed] louse.

Sue a beggar and catch/get a louse.

Mackerel

Throw out a sprat to catch a mackerel.

Mare

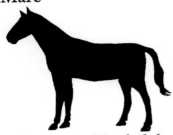

See also colt, filly, foal, horse, jade, stallion, steed.

A mare's shoe and a horse's shoe are both alike.

All is well, and the man has his mare again. (8)

He that lacks my mare may buy my mare.

How can the foal amble if the horse and mare trot?

It is hard to make an old mare leave flinging [kicking].

Money makes the mare to go.

My old mare would have a new crupper.

Nothing so bold as a blind mare.

Put the man to the mear [mare] that can manage the mear. (15)

Ride a horse and mare on the shoulders, an ass and mule on the buttocks.

Ride who will, the mare is shod.

The blind mare is first in the mire.

The grey mare is the better horse. (i.e. The mare signifies the wife.)

The kick of the mare hurts not the colt.

The man shall have his mare again. (1)

The smith's mare and the cobbler's wife are always the worst shod.

The three most fortunate things a man ever had; a mare, a sow and a goose (7).

When the mare has a bald face the filly will have a blaze. (i.e. A white mark on its face.)

Martin

The robin and the wren are God's cock and hen, the martin and the swallow are God's bow and arrow. (1)

The robin/sparrow and the wren are God's cock and hen: the martin and the swallow are God's mate and marrow [companion].

The sparrow builds in the martin's nest. (8)

Mastiff

See also bitch, cur, dog, greyhound, hound, pup, spaniel, whelp.

A mastiff grows the fiercer for being tied up.

Though the mastiff be gentle, yet bite him not by the lip.

Yelping curs may anger mastiffs at last./Yelping curs will raise mastiffs.

Midge

The mother of mischief is no bigger than a midge's wing.

The moudiewart [mole] feedsna [feeds not] on midges.

Mole

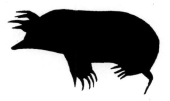

A mole wants no lanthorn.

The moudiewart [mole] feedsna [feeds not] on midges.

Monkey

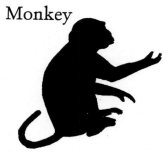

See also ape.

Every monkey will have his gambols. (8)

If you pay peanuts, you get monkeys. (17)

The higher the monkey climbs/goes, the more he shows his tail.

Moth

The best cloth may have a moth in it. (8)

Mouse

A blate [shy] cat makes a proud mouse.

A dead mouse feels no cold./Dead mice feel no cold.

A lion may (come to) be beholden to a mouse.

A mouse in time may bite a cable in two/in two a cable.

A mouse may help a lion.

A wee mouse will creep beneath a muckle [big] corn stack.

Be either a man or a mouse. (9)

Better a mouse in the pot than no flesh at all. (Italian) (11)

Burn not your house to fright [frighten] away the mice./Burn not your house to fright the mouse away.

Can a mouse fall in love with a cat? (8)

Don't let the plough stand to kill a mouse./Let not the plough stand to kill a mouse.

Don't make yourself a mouse, or the cat will eat you. (16)

He who lives with cats will get a taste for mice. (4)

I would rather hear the lark sing than the mouse cheep./It is better to hear the lark sing than the mouse cheep/chirp.

If the cat sits long enough at the hole she will catch the mouse.

If the frog and the mouse quarrel, the kite will see them agreed.

In baiting a mousetrap with cheese, always leave room for the mouse. (Greek) (11)

It is a bold/wily mouse that breeds/nestles in the cat's ear.

It is needless to pour water on a drowned mouse.

It's a mean mouse that has but ae [one] hole. (10)

It's a sair [sore] time when the mouse looks out o' the meal barrel wi' a tear in its e'e [eye].

Keep no more cats than will catch mice.

Let the cat wink, and let the mouse run.

Loud cheeps the mouse when the cat's no rustling.

Mice care not to play with kittens. (8)

No larder but has its mice. (4)

One for the mouse, one for the crow, one to rot, and one to grow.

Silence catches/grips a/the mouse.

The cats that drive the mice away are as good as they that catch them. (German) (11)

The escaped mouse ever feels the taste of the bait.

The mouse lordships where a cat is not. (8)

The mouse that has but one hole is quickly taken.

Though thy enemy seem a mouse, yet watch him like a lion.

Today a man, tomorrow a mouse.

Two cats and a mouse, two wives in one house, two dogs and a bone, never agree in one.

Well kens the mouse when the cat's out of the house.

What would a young cat do but eat mice/kill a mouse. (Irish)

When the cat is out the mouse can dance./When the cat's away the mice may/will play.

When the cat winks, little wots the mouse what the cat thinks.

Who takes a lion when he is absent, fears a mouse present. (4)

Mule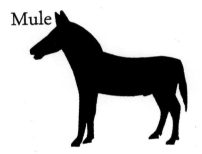

See also ass, donkey.

He who wants a mule without fault, must walk on foot.

One mule scrubs another.

Ride a horse and mare on the shoulders, an ass and mule on the buttocks.

Mussel

There's life in a mussel as lang [long] as it can cheep [squeak].

When the pea's in bloom the mussel's toom [empty].

Newt

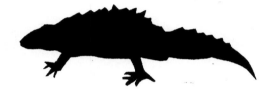

All that breed in the mud are not efts [newts]. (15)

Nightingale

Nightingales can sing their own song best. (8)

On the third of April come the cuckoo and nightingale.

The nightingale and cuckoo sing both in one month.

When the owl sings, the nightingale will hold her peace. (15)

Owl

An ass is the gravest beast, an owl the gravest bird. (8)

An/the owl is the king of the night.

He is in great want of a bird that will give a groat for an owl.

I have lived too near a wood to be frightened by owls. (15)/I live too near a wood to be scared by owls. (Greek) (11)

The ignorant have an eagle's wings and an owl's eyes.

The owl thinks her own young fairest./ The owl thinks all her young ones beauties.

When the owl sings, the nightingale will hold her peace. (15)

Ox

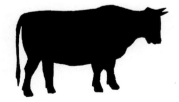

See also bull, calf, cattle, cow, heifer.

A lazy ox is little better for the goad.

A man must plough with such oxen as he has.

An old ox makes/ploughs a straight furrow.

An old ox will find (a) shelter for himself.

An ox is taken by his horns, and a man by his word. (4)

An ox is taken by his horns, and a man by the tongue.

An ox, when he is loose, licks himself at pleasure.

Beauty draws more than (five yokes of) oxen.

Better an egg in peace than an ox in war. (4)

Fling at the brod [goad] was ne'er a good ox.

He that sows in the highway tires his oxen and loses his corn.

He that will steal an egg will steal an ox.

He who greases his wheels helps his oxen.

If the ox fall, whet your knife. (8)/When the ox stumbles, all whet their knives. (Yiddish) (11)

Nature draws more than ten oxen. (1)

Ne'er put the plough before the owsen [oxen]. (10)

Old oxen have stiff horns.

The ox is never woe, till he to the harrow go.

The ox when weariest treads surest./The tired ox treads surest.

The stolen ox sometimes puts his head out of the stall. (Spanish) (11)

Where shall the ox go but he must labour. (1)/Whither shall the ox go where he shall not labour?

Oyster

He was a bold man that first ate an oyster.

Oysters are only in season in the R. months./Oysters are only in season in those months that are spell'd with an R.

Partridge

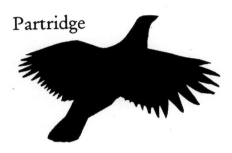

If the partridge had the woodcock's thigh, it would be the best bird that ever did fly.

Peacock

"Fly pride," says the peacock.

March comes in with adder heads, and goes out with peacock tails.

No peacock envies another peacock his tail. (Latin)

The peacock cries before the rain. (8)

The peacock has fair feathers but foul feet.

The sparrow is sorry for the peacock at the burden of its tail. (11)

When the peacock loudly bawls, soon we'll have both rain and squalls./When the peacock loudly calls, then look out for storms and squalls. (11)

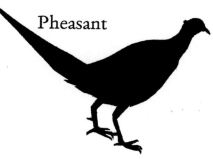

Pheasant

A sparrow in hand is worth a pheasant that flieth by. (8)

Pheasants are fools if they invite the hawk to dinner. (8)

Pig

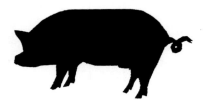

See also hog, sow, swine.

A barren sow was never good to pigs.

A pig that has two owners is sure to die of hunger. (11)

A pretty pig makes an ugly (old) sow.

Don't give cherries to pigs; don't give advice to a fool./Neither give cherries to pigs nor advice to a fool.

He that loves noise must buy a pig.

If you catch a pig catch it by the leg. (7)

Lead a pig to the Rhine, it remains a pig. (4)

Never buy a pig in a poke. (16)

One pig knows another. (7)

Pigs grow fat where lambs would starve. (11)

Pigs may whistle, but they hae [have] an ill [bad] mouth for't.

Pigs might fly, but they are most/very unlikely birds.

Pigs might fly, if they had wings. (4)

Pigs see the wind.

Pigs won't thrive on clean water. (18)

The first pig, but the last whelp of the litter, is the best.

The quiet pigs eat all the draff. (7)

The world's quiet and the pig is in the sty. (7)

The worst pig often gets the best pear.

The young pig grunts like the old sow.

What can you expect from a pig but a grunt?

When pigs carry sticks, the clouds will play tricks, when they lie in the mud, no fear of a flood. (11)

You cannot make a horn of a pig's tail.

Pigeon

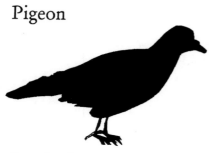

See also dove.

Better a sparrow in the hand than a pigeon on the roof. (4)

Full pigeons find cherries bitter.

Roasted pigeons will not fly into one's mouth. (Dutch) (11)

Pigeons are taken when crows fly at pleasure. (8)

The pigeon never knows woe, but when she does a-benting go. (i.e. Feeding on grass seeds.)

When the pigeons go abenting, (then) the farmers go/lie lamenting.

Pike

Better be the head of a pike than the tail of a sturgeon.

Plover

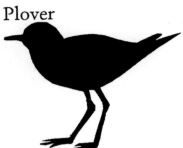

It's a long way from home that the plover cries. (7)

When plovers do fast appear, it shows that frosts are very near, but when the plovers thus do go, then you may look for heavy snow. (11)

Porpoise

The porpoise plays before a storm. (15)

Pullet

See also chicken, cock, fowl, hen.

A pullet in the pen is worth a hundred in the fen.

Pup(py)

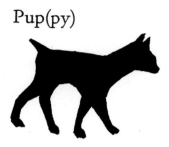

See also bitch, cur, dog, greyhound, hound, mastiff, spaniel, whelp.

A wonder lasts but nine days, and then the puppy's een [eyes] are open. (9)

Every hound is a pup till he hunts. (7)

Rabbit

If three dogs chase a rabbit they cannot kill it. (11)

Ram

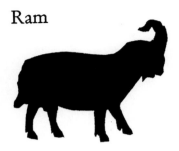

See also ewe, lamb, sheep, wether.

A pet lamb makes a cross ram. (11)

He that would have his fold full, must keep an old tup [ram] and a young bull. (8)

Rat

An old rat is a brave rat. (11)

Put an old cat to an old rat. (15)

Rats desert/forsake/leave a falling house.

Rats desert a sinking ship.

The last kick of a dying rat is always the worst. (18)

The rat that has but ae [one] hole is soon catch'd. (9)

To a good rat, a good cat. (11)

Too many cats are worse than rats. (18)

"Welcome death," quoth the rat, when the trap fell down.

Raven

Corbies [ravens] dinna gather without they smell carrion. (10)

Corbies [ravens] dinna [do not] pick out corbies' een [eyes].

He that takes the raven for his guide will light on carrion.

Raise ravens and they will peck out your eyes. (Spanish) (11)

The croaking raven bodes misfortune. (i.e. death) (15)

The raven chides blackness. (8)

To the raven her own chick is white./The raven thinks its own chick white/dear.

Where the carcass is, the ravens will gather.

Robin

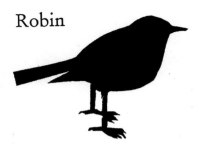

He that hurts a robin will never prosper. (11)

If/when the robin sings in the bush, then the weather will be coarse; but if the robin sings in/on the barn, then the weather will be warm.

The robin and the wren are God's cock and hen, the martin and the swallow are God's bow and arrow. (1)/The robin and the wren are God's cock and hen: the martin and the swallow are God's mate and marrow [companion].

Rook

Ding [knock]down the nests, and the rooks will flee away. (12)

Salmon

A hook's well lost to catch a salmon.
A trout in the ashes is better than a salmon in the water. (18)
A trout in the pot is better than a salmon in the sea.
Salmon and sermon have their season in Lent.
Seven herrings are a meal for a salmon. (18)
'Tis not for everyone to catch a salmon. (8)

Scorpion

There is/sleeps a scorpion under every stone.

Serpent

See also adder, snake, viper.

He that has been bitten by a serpent is afraid of a rope. (4)

It is good to strike the serpent's head with your enemy's hand.

Serpents engender in still waters. (8)

The tongue is more venomous than a serpent's sting. (4)

Whom a serpent has bitten, a lizard alarms.

Sheep

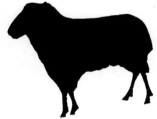

See also ewe, lamb, ram, wether.

A bleating sheep loses a bit/bite.

A good man can no more harm than a sheep. (4)

A good shepherd must fleece his sheep, not flay them. (15)

A lamb when carried far becomes as burdensome as a sheep. (14)

A lazy sheep thinks its wool heavy.

A leap year is never a good sheep year.

A soft-dropping April brings milk to cows and sheep. (7)

As soon goes the young sheep to the pot as the old.

Better give the wool than the sheep. (15)

By little and little the wolf eats (up) the sheep.

Carrion crows bewail the dead sheep, and then eat them.

Death devours lambs as well as sheep.

Don't go putting wool on the sheep's back. (18)

Every scabby sheep likes a comrade. (18)/There was never a scabby sheep in a flock that didn't like to have a comrade.[*]

Go to law for a sheep and lose your cow. (4)

He that has sheep, swine, and bees, sleep he, wake he, he may thrive.

He that has one sheep in the flock will like all the rest the better for it.

He that makes himself a sheep shall be eaten by the wolf.

Idle dogs worry sheep.

If one sheep leap o'er the dyke, all the rest will follow.

If one sheep puts his head through the gap the rest will follow.(18)

It is a foolish sheep that makes the wolf his/its confessor.

It never troubles a wolf how many the sheep be.

Let every sheep hang by his/its own shank.

Now I have a sheep and a cow and everyone bids me "Good morrow".

One foolish sheep will lead the flock. (11)

One scabbed sheep will mar a whole flock./One scabby sheep infects/spoils a whole flock.

One sheep follows another.

Shear your sheep when elder blossoms peep. (11)

---

[*] *Irish Proverbs*, Appletree Press

Sike [such] as the shepherd, sike be his sheep. (15)

Tethered sheep will not thrive. (18)

The dust raised by the sheep does not choke the wolf.

The lamb is a sheep in the long run. (7)

The lone sheep is in danger of the wolf.

The wolf eats often of the sheep that have been told/warned.

There are black sheep in every flock/fold./There is a black sheep in every flock.

Twa [two] wolfs [wolves] may worrie [worry] ane [one] sheep.

When sheep and lambs do gambol and fight, the weather will change before the night. (11)

When the cuckoo comes to the bare thorn, sell your cow and buy your corn; but when she comes to the full bit, sell your corn and buy your sheep.

Where every hand fleeces, the sheep goes naked.

Wolves rend sheep when shepherds fail.

Snail

Pains and patience would take a snail to America. (18)

The snail slides up the tower at last, though the swallow mounteth it sooner.

Time and patience would bring the snail to Jerusalem. (7)

Tramp [tread] on a snail, and she'll shoot out her horns.

When black snails on the road you see, then on the morrow rain will be.

Snake

See also adder, serpent, viper.

Take heed of the snake in the grass. (16)

There is no bite to the old snake. (8)

Snipe

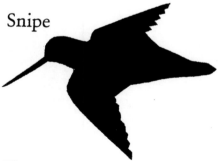

The snite [snipe] need not the woodcock betwite [upbraid].

There is winter enough for the snipe and woodcock too.

You can't check a snipe for having a long bill. (18)

Sow

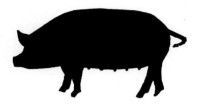

See also hog, pig, swine.

A barren sow was never good to pigs.

A pretty pig makes an ugly (old) sow.

A sow may whistle, though it has an ill mouth for it. (17)

A/the still sow eats (up) all the draff.

Dirty troughs will serve dirty sows. (8)

Every sow to her own trough.

It is not the big sow that eats the most. (18)

It would be a hard task to follow a black dockit [docked] sow through a burnt moor this night. (10)

Little knows the fat sow, what the lean one means.

Silence in the pig market, and let the old sow have a grunt. (15)

The sow reeks not of balm. (15)

The three most fortunate things a man ever had; a mare, a sow and a goose. (7)

The young pig grunts like the old sow.

"There's an unco [strange] splutter," quo' the sow i' the gutter. (10)

You cannot/can't make a silk purse out of a sow's ear.

Spaniel

See also bitch, cur, dog, greyhound, hound, mastiff, pup, whelp.

Spaniels that fawn when beaten will never forsake their masters.

Sparrow

A sparrow in hand is worth a pheasant that flieth by. (8)

Auld [old] sparrows are ill to tame.

Better a sparrow in the hand than a pigeon on the roof. (4)

Every sparrow to its ear of wheat. (8)

The sparrow and the wren are God's cock and hen: the martin and the swallow are God's mate and marrow. (companion)

The sparrow builds in the martin's nest. (8)

The sparrow is sorry for the peacock at the burden of its tail. (11)

Two sparrows on one ear of corn make an ill agreement./Two sparrows upon one ear of wheat cannot agree.

Spider

If you want/wish to live and thrive, let a/the spider run alive.

Spider lost her distaff, and is ever since forced to draw her thread through her tail. (15)

Spider's webs floating at an autumn sunset bring a night frost. (11)

Where the bee sucks honey, the spider sucks poison.

Sprat

Every sprat nowadays calls itself a herring.

Often a man cast a sprat to catch a hake. (Irish)

Throw out a sprat to catch a mackerel.

Squirrel

You must hunt squirrels and make no noise.

Stallion

See also colt, filly, foal, horse, jade, mare, steed.

Do not mistake a goat's beard for a fine stallion's tail.[*]

---

[*] *Irish Proverbs*, Appletree Press

Steed

See also colt, filly, foal, horse, jade, mare, stallion.

It is too late to shut the stable-door when the steed is stolen./When the steed is stolen, shut the stable-door.

While the grass grows, the steed starves. (17)

Sturgeon

Better be the head of a pike than the tail of a sturgeon.

Swallow

One swallow does not make a summer.

One swallow makes not a spring, nor a woodcock a winter. (11)

The robin and the wren are God's cock and hen, the martin and the swallow are God's bow and arrow. (1)

The robin and the wren are God's cock and hen: the martin and the swallow are God's mate and marrow [companion].

The snail slides up the tower at last, though the swallow mounteth it sooner.

You can't teach a swallow how to fly. (18)

Swan

The swan sings before death. (1)

The swan sings when death comes.

Swine

See also hog, pig, sow.

A swine over fat, is the cause of his own bane.

Do not throw pearls to swine./Don't cast your pearls before swine.

Draff [hogwash] is good enough for swine.

He that has sheep, swine, and bees, sleep he, wake he, he may thrive.

Still swine eat all the draff [hogwash].

Thrush

A thrush paid for is better than a turkey owing for. (8)

He that has patience, has fat thrushes for a farthing. (4)

If wishes were thrushes, then beggars would eat birds.

The thrush, avoiding the trap, fell into birdlime. (8)

Tick

An/the empty tick sucks sore.

Tiger

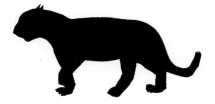

He who rides a tiger is afraid to dismount./He who rides the tiger can never dismount. (Chinese) (11)

Those who hunt deer sometimes raise tigers. (Indian) (11)

Unless you enter the tiger's den you cannot take the cubs. (Japanese) (11)

Toad

Gentle puddocks [toads] have long toes.

The toad said to the harrow, "Cursed be so many lords." (15)

Tortoise

The tortoise wins the race while the hare is sleeping.

Trout

A trout in the ashes is better than a salmon in the water. (18)

A trout in the pot is better than a salmon in the sea.

Every fisher loves best the trout that is of his own tickling. (11)

Listen to the sound of the river and you will catch a trout. (Irish)

Said the chevin [chub] to the trout, "My head's worth all thy bonk [body]". (8)

There's no catching trouts with dry breeches. (Portuguese) (11)

When trout refuse bait or fly, storm it is that now is nigh. (11)

You must lose a fly to catch a trout.

Turkey

A thrush paid for is better than a turkey owing for. (8)

Viper

See also adder, serpent, snake.
No viper so little, but has its venom.

Wasp

Wasps haunt the honey-pot. (8)

Weasel

When the weasel and the cat make a marriage, it is a very ill [bad] presage.

Wether

See also ewe, lamb, ram, sheep.

Give never the wolf the wether to keep.

Let aye [always] the belled wether break the snow. (4)

Whelp

See also bitch, dog, fox, greyhound, hound, lion, mastiff, spaniel.

Destroy the lion while he is but/yet a whelp.

Give the bairn/child his will, and a whelp his fill, and neither/none of these two will thrive.

The first pig, but the last whelp of the litter, is the best.

The hasty bitch brings forth blind whelps.

The hungry hound thinks not of her whelps. (7)

The tod's [fox's] bairns [whelps] are ill to tame.

We may not expect a good whelp from an ill [bad] dog.

Wolf

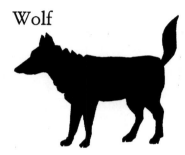

A growing youth has a wolf in his belly.

A thief knows a thief as a wolf knows a wolf.

As a wolf is like a dog, so is a flatterer like a friend.

Asses die and wolves bury them. (8)

By little and little the wolf eats (up) the goose/sheep.

Give never the wolf the wether to keep.

He that makes himself a sheep shall be eaten by the wolf.

Hunger drives/fetches the wolf out of the wood.

If you cut down the woods, you'll catch the wolf.

Ill herds make fat wolves. (i.e. Carelessness gives occasion to steal.)

It is a foolish sheep that makes the wolf his/its confessor.

It is/'Tis a hard winter when one wolf eats another.

It never troubles a wolf how many the sheep be.

Man is a wolf to man. (Latin)

No matter how much you feed a wolf he will always return to the forest. (Russian) (11)

One must howl with the wolves.

The death of a young wolf never comes too soon.

The death of the wolves is the safety of the sheep.

The dust raised by the sheep does not choke the wolf.

The kid that keeps above is in no danger of the wolf.

The life of the wolf is the death of the lamb. (15)

The lone sheep is in danger of the wolf.

The moon does not heed the barking of wolves.

The wolf and fox are both of one counsel. (15)

The wolf changes his coat but not his nature. (Latin)

The wolf eats often of the sheep that have been told/warned.

The wolf knows what the ill beast thinks.

The wolf may lose his teeth, but never his nature./The wolf loses his teeth, but not his inclinations. (Spanish) (11)

The wolf must die in his own skin.

The wolf preys farthest from his den. (15)

Twa [two] wolfs [wolves] may worrie [harrass] ane [one] sheep. (4)

When the wolf comes in at the door, love creeps out of the window. (16)

While you trust the dog, the wolf slips into the sheepfold.

Who keeps company with the wolf, will learn to howl.

Who speaks of the wolf sees his tail. (8)

Wolves lose their teeth, but not their memory. (8)

Wolves rend sheep when shepherds fail. (15)

Woodcock

If the partridge had the woodcock's thigh, it would be the best bird that ever did fly.

One woodcock does not make a winter.

The snite [snipe] need not the woodcock betwite [upbraid].

There is winter enough for the snipe and woodcock too.

Woodlark

A goshawk beats not at a bunting [woodlark].

Worm

Even a worm will turn.

The early bird catches the worm./'Tis the early bird that catches the worm.

Tramp [tread] on a worm and it will stir its tail. (9)

Tread on a worm and it will turn.

Wren

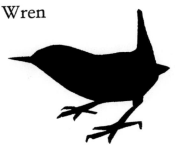

A wren in the hand is better than a crane to be caught. (7)

As sore fight wrens as cranes.

He that hurts robin or wren, will never prosper, boy nor man. (8)

Kill a wren but beware of fire. (7)

The robin and the wren are God's cock and hen, the martin and the swallow are God's bow and arrow. (1)

The robin/sparrow and the wren are God's cock and hen: the martin and the swallow are God's mate and marrow [companion].

Wrens may prey where eagles dare not perch. (8)

Bibliography

(1)   Browning, D.C.   *Everyman's Dictionary of Quotations and Proverbs*, J.M. Dent & Sons Ltd, London 1951.

(1)   Collins, V.H.   *A Book of English Proverbs*, Longman, London 1972.

(3)   Evans, I.H. (Revised by)   *Brewer's Dictionary of Phrase and Fable*, Cassell Publishers Ltd, London 1990.

(4)   Fergusson, D.   *Fergusson's Scottish Proverbs from the Original Print of 1641*, William Blackwood and Sons, Edinburgh and London 1924.

(5)   Fergusson, R.   *The Penguin Dictionary of Proverbs*(Penguin Books, 1983), copyright (c) Market House Books, Harmondsworth 1986.

(6)   Flavell, L. & R.   *Dictionary of Proverbs and Their Origins*, Kyle Cathie Limited, London 1993.

(7)   Gaffney, S. & Cashamn, S. (Edited by)   *Proverbs and Sayings of Ireland*, Wolfhound Press, Dublin 1979.

(8)   Hazlitt, W.C.   *English Proverbs and Proverbial Phrases*, Reeves & Turner, 1882 and 1917.

(9)   Henderson, A.   *Scottish Proverbs*, Oliver & Boyd, Edinburgh 1832.

(10)   Hislop, A.   *The Proverbs of Scotland*, Porteous & Hislop, Glasgow 1862.

(11) Houghton, P.   *The Cassell Book of Proverbs,* Cassell
                          Publishers Ltd, Villiers House,
                          London 1992.

(12) Kelly, J.   *A Complete Collection of Scottish
                          Proverbs*, London, William and John
                          Innys and John Osborn, 1721.

(13) Marshall, S.   *Under the Hawthorn,*, J.M. Dent &
                          Sons Ltd, London 1981.

(14) O'Rahilly, T.F.   *A Miscellany of Irish Proverbs*,
      M.A., (Collected   The Talbot Press, Dublin 1922.
      and edited by)

(15) Smith, W. G.   *The Oxford Dictionary of English
      (compiled by)   Proverbs*, Oxford University Press,
      Wilson, F.P.   Oxford 1970.
      (Revised by)

(16) Ridout, R. &   *English Proverbs Explained*,
      Witting, C.   Heinemann, London 1967.

(17) Simpson, J.   *The Concise Oxford Dictionary of
                          Proverbs*, Oxford University Press,
                          Oxford 1987.

(18) Williams, F.   *The Poolbeg Book of Irish Proverbs*,
                          Poolbeg Press Ltd, Swords, Ireland
                          1992.

      Bailey, K.   *Irish Proverbs*, Appletree Press Ltd,
      (Illustrated by)   Belfast 1987.